My Book of Islamic Rhymes

by

Rashid Ahmad Chaudhry

ISLAM INTERNATIONAL PUBLICATIONS LTD.

My Book of Islamic Rhymes

Written by Rashid Ahmad Chaudhry

First published in UK, 2008 (ISBN: 185372688-5)
Reprinted (with a new format) in the UK, 2016

Published by
Islam International Publications Ltd.
(Additional Wakaalat-e-Tasneef)
Islamabad, Sheephatch Lane
Tilford, Surrey GU10 2AQ, UK

For further information please visit www.alislam.org.

ISBN 978-1-84880-870-6
10 9 8 7 6 5 4 3 2

Contents

In the name of Allah, Most Gracious, Ever Merciful

Foreword

'My Book of Islamic Rhymes' is another addition to the series of books published by the Children's Book Committee. This book aims to give our young readers an introduction to Islam and its values in a series of short rhymes. We hope that both parents and children will welcome this publication, and that this book will inspire our young readers to behave in accordance with the wonderful teachings of Islam.

The Children's Book Committee was set up under the supervision and guidance of Hazrat Khalifatul-Masih IV[rta] and continued to receive support and guidance from Hazrat Khalifatul-Masih V[aba]. The Late Rashid Ahmad Chaudhry was the first Chairman of this Committee; he held this post from the inception of the Committee in 1984 until his death in December 2005. The poetry in this book is his work and was edited by the members of the Children's Book Committee.

In the present edition, activities for children have been added at the end of each Rhyme, prepared by Haallah Ahmad (Shams); whereas corrections and checking of script was done by Naseer-ud-Din Shams. Layout and formatting was done by Shaikh Naseer Ahmad, and Ata-ul-Aziz. May Allah bless all of those involved in

the publication of this book for their dedication and hard work
and reward them abundantly in this world and the Hereafter.
Aameen.

Munir-ud-Din Shams
Additional Wakeelut-Tasneef,
August, 2016

We Promise

We promise that we'll speak the truth
   We promise that we'll never lie

We promise that we'll live for our Faith
   We promise that for Islam we'll try

We promise that we'll obey our parents
   And treat them well as years go by

We promise that we'll be kind to youngsters
   And promise not to make them cry

We promise we won't be rude to teachers
   And their orders we'll never defy

We promise that we'll acquire knowledge
   To keep on learning and never be shy

We promise to worship Allah alone
   On His guidance we'll always rely

We promise that we'll be good citizens
   And every rule we'll abide by

We promise to acquire all true virtues
  And all our mistakes we'll rectify

We promise that we'll help the poor
  And in their hour of need we'll stand by

We promise we'll never think of rest
  Till Islam's banner is raised up high

With our hearts we'll obey our Leader
  And we'll never ever ask him why

We know that we are Ahmadi Muslims
  We know God is with us and close by

We know that enemies can't harm us
  No matter how hard they may try

We know the days are fast approaching
  When the truth of Islam no-one can deny

We promise we are Ahmadi Muslims
  To be the best we will always vie

ACTIVITY

Choose one promise that you personally want to work on to help better yourself. Write an action plan to help you keep the promise:

E.g. The promise I want to work on is .... helping the poor

My Action Plan is ...I will be more mindful about giving to someone in need, even if it is just a smile. ☺

The promise I want to work on is _____

_____

_____

_____

My action plan is _____

_____

_____

_____

_____

_____

_____

_____

_____

_____

_____

_____

_____

_____

Murabbi Sahib

Murabbi Sahib, Murabbi Sahib, have you any time?
  To teach me Arabic properly and the meaning of the Quran?

Murabbi Sahib, Murabbi Sahib, have you any time?
  To show me how to offer my Prayers and stand to call out Adhan?

Murabbi Sahib, Murabbi Sahib, have you any time?
  To relate stories of the Holy Prophet^(saw) and the Messiah^(as) from Qadian?

Murabbi Sahib, Murabbi Sahib, have you any time?
  To explain the philosophy of Fasting and blessings of Ramadan?

Murabbi Sahib, Murabbi Sahib, have you any time?
  To teach me the Five Pillars and the articles of Imaan?

Murabbi Sahib, Murabbi Sahib, have you any time?
  To show me the wonderful beauties of the religion called Islam?

ACTIVITY

Murabbis have a wealth of knowledge that they have acquired over many years. If you have a local Murabbi, ask them questions both religious and non religious. For example you could ask them why they wanted to become a Murabbi, what they had to do in order to become a Murabbi, what their daily routine consists of, what their favourite food is, or whether they have any hobbies, etc. Don't forget to thank them for all the sacrifices that they make for our Jama'at.

What I found out from my local Murabbi Sahib is ___

_____

_____

_____

_____

_____

_____

_____

_____

_____

_____

_____

_____

_____

_____

_____

_____

True Muslims

All praise is due to Allah
　　To Him alone do we pray.

With all our heart we love Him
　　And all His commands we obey.

We always seek His guidance
　　In our work and in our play.

We are indeed true Muslims
　　We always do as we say.

Our Khalifah is amongst us
　　How can we go astray?

We are willing to devote
　　Our lives in Allah's way.

Armed with the help of Allah
　　Through darkness we find our way

With the Grace of Allah Almighty
　　From evils we will turn away.

ACTIVITY

Unscramble the words below from the poem:

Y	B	O	E		H	L	L	A	A		N	D	A

	I	H	S		L	K	A	A	I	H	F	H	.

		R	O	U		E	R	S	H	T	A

I	L	I	W		U	N	T	R		Y	A	A	W

	R	M	O	F		K	S	N	D	E	A	S	R

	D	A	N		L	S	V	E	I	.

CHALLENGE: We are so fortunate to be a part of the Ahmadiyya Muslim Community! Regardless of where we live, we can make a personal bond with Huzoor by writing to him on a regular basis. Try to write to Huzoor at least once a month. Keep a log so you can look back and see whether you managed to complete this challenge!

MY LOG FOR WRITING TO HUZOOR

Tick **YES** or **NO** if you managed to write to Huzoor each month. If you ticked YES, write how many times you wrote during that month.

MONTH	YES	NO	TIMES
JANUARY			
FEBRUARY			
MARCH			
APRIL			
MAY			
JUNE			
JULY			
AUGUST			
SEPTEMBER			
OCTOBER			
NOVEMBER			
DECEMBER			

Next year, try to improve on this log ☺.

The Promised Messiah, may peace be on him

The sun has now darkened
  The moon has lost its light
For the appearance of the Mahdi^{as}
  The time was completely right.

Tis said in the Bible
  These signs would come about
For the advent of Prophet Jesus^{as}
  So there could be no doubt.

The sun has now eclipsed
  And the moon has eclipsed too
Both happened in the month of fasting
  Normally they never do.

According to the writings
  Before this very sign
The Promised Messiah^{as} the Imam Mahdi
  Would have announced his design.

This sign as you well know
  Appeared in 1894
Unique was this occurrence as it had
  A sign from Allah Almighty
  For both the rich and the poor

To look for the claimant
    You should seriously try
I am sure you will find him
    If you have spiritual eyes

Listen to mother earth
    Pay heed to the skies
Hear the words of the ancient scriptures
    The heavens cannot lie

Accept the Messiah, the Imam Mahdi
    Like others have done too
Come on now, do not hesitate
    Come start your life anew

Ghulam Ahmad[as] his name
    And his birth town Qadian
'Ismohu Ahmad' His name is Ahmad[as]
    Is mentioned in the Quran

The Messiah has now come
    With true power and glory
So recognise and accept him now
    Or you'll be forever sorry

ACTIVITY

Let's see if you can find all of the words!

A	L	L	A	H	H	S	F	J	X	L	D	J	K	X	L	I
E	B	I	B	L	E	E	M	Q	V	F	A	U	J	H	Y	Z
M	F	A	V	P	N	R	E	G	U	T	M	S	W	K	H	M
O	S	I	D	N	M	U	C	Y	Q	R	H	T	B	W	P	M
N	A	U	L	A	H	T	L	R	A	J	A	D	F	X	U	L
T	D	N	N	H	I	P	I	L	K	E	M	N	B	H	N	V
H	L	Y	H	Q	M	I	P	I	Y	S	A	R	X	A	I	I
O	U	W	G	M	A	R	S	D	F	U	L	Q	L	I	Q	N
F	D	D	E	I	M	C	E	F	Y	S	U	W	A	S	U	D
F	T	A	N	H	M	S	D	N	A	P	H	R	U	S	E	L
A	W	Z	O	T	A	T	H	S	D	W	G	A	T	E	S	M
S	Q	P	O	P	H	N	X	S	V	E	N	U	I	M	X	H
T	D	Y	M	E	D	E	N	N	E	V	Z	A	R	E	N	I
I	S	R	H	C	I	I	Z	Z	N	W	N	Z	I	R	J	T
N	A	P	L	C	A	C	O	K	T	W	U	Z	P	D	Y	R
G	U	O	S	A	M	N	D	J	G	I	T	C	S	E	A	G
B	S	Q	D	U	G	A	P	J	C	E	H	B	E	O	H	Q

Find these words in the word search:

ALLAH	BIBLE	ADVENT
SPIRITUAL	MONTH OF FASTING	QADIAN
JESUS	ANCIENT SCRIPTURES	MESSIAH
UNIQUE	SUN	IMAM MAHDI
LIFE	MOON	GHULAM AHMAD
QURAN	ECLIPSED	ACCEPT HIM

CHALLENGE: All the major religions are still waiting for their foretold Messiah to appear. In fact many Muslims are still awaiting the coming of the Messiah. Ahmadi Muslims are the only people today that believe the Messiah has already come; the founder of the Ahmadiyya Muslim Community, Hazrat Mirza Ghulam Ahmad of Qadian—we believe that he is the Messiah that all religions are awaiting.

Go to the official Jama'at website: www.alislam.org. Research the eclipse of the sun and the moon as a sign for the coming of the awaited Messiah and Mahdi. Write down in your own words what the sign was and why it is so important:

_____

_____

_____

_____

_____

_____

_____

_____

_____

_____

_____

_____

_____

_____

EXTENSION CHALLENGE: Do you know any of the other signs for the coming of the Messiah and Mahdi? Try to research this too:

_____
_____
_____
_____
_____
_____
_____
_____
_____
_____
_____
_____
_____
_____
_____
_____
_____
_____
_____
_____
_____
_____
_____

Ahmadi Muslim Children

Ahmadi Muslim children
  Get up before dawn
Whether in London
  Or in Qadian

They go to the mosque
  When the Adhan is heard
They offer their Prayers
  Not uttering a word

They recite the Quran
  With a voice loud and clear
To them this Holy book
  Is so very dear

They believe the Quran
  Is God's Word alone
Sent down to us all
  From His majestic Throne

They believe that Muhammad^{saw}
  Is the saviour of mankind
And the religion of Islam
  Is the best for the mind

They try their utmost
　　To please their Great Lord
And do all good deeds
　　Without any rewards

They lead their whole life
　　To the Lord's teachings
And are ever ready
　　In the field of preaching

They always study hard
　　But also enjoy their play
Their aim is very high
　　They worship God everyday

They are athletic in body
　　Sharp in mind and wit
A good sense of humour
　　All part of their toolkit

Kind to the young ones
　　Obedient to their parents
They are gentle in friendship
　　But severe to opponents

Moderation in everything
　　For them it's the key
Not too much, nor too little
　　Stops them from being greedy

'As-Siddiq,' the Truthful
    The Trustworthy, 'al-Ameen,'
Is what they endeavour
    For themselves to be

For the sake of their faith
    They are ready to sacrifice
Time, honour and wealth
    Throughout their whole life

They love Khilafat-e-Ahmadiyya
    Hazrat Ameer-ul-Momineen[aba]
To obey all his commands
    They are forever keen

ACTIVITY

This poem mentions many qualities of being an Ahmadi Muslim. Using your own life experiences, write a poem detailing the qualities you have that make you a great Ahmadi Muslim! You can choose your own title or you can use this one:

I AM AN AHMADI MUSLIM.

_____

_____

_____

_____

_____

_____

_____

_____

_____

_____

_____

_____

_____

_____

_____

_____.

A Pious Man's Vision

A pious man was praying one night
*   When he saw a vision, an angel bright*

The angel said to him, 'Do you know
*   What's happening in the town below'*

The pious man then said, 'I confess
*   Whatever they do, I cannot guess'*

The angel said, 'Come along with me,
*   I will take you around the whole city'*

They both travelled along in the dark
*   Through streets, homes and even the park*

Together they saw many people within
*   Who were completely engaged in vice and sin*

The pious man was very much grieved
*   Deep in his heart he almost believed*

That because of this disgusting sight
*   Evil would destroy this city tonight*

He poured his heart before God and prayed
*   He prayed and he prayed that the city be saved*

He resolved that he would not rest
  Against these evils he would do his best

Sometime later, again the angel came
  And spoke to the man who was still feeling shame

They both set out for another round
  And walked the streets without any sound

This time they saw quite a different sight
  Opposite to what they saw at night

There were now people praying to God
  Supplicating before their Good Lord

Rushing to the mosque in the freezing cold
  Some were little ones while some were old

On their lips, many songs of praises
  Uttering humbly thanksgiving phrases

Some were engaged in beautiful recitation
  Of the Holy Quran, and others in meditation

The pious man was now satisfied
  With joy in his heart he almost cried

Finding people living in this city
  Who worship God and proudly declare

'With all our force we will surely fight
    And crush the evil with all our might'

Seeing their resolve and determination
    Remarked the angel, 'What a creation!'

God the Almighty will hear their call
    And His mercy will cover them all

ACTIVITY

Draw a picture of the town described in this poem before the pious mans prayers, then draw a picture of the same town after the pious mans prayers:

Town before prayers

Town after prayers

WHO OR WHAT DO YOU PRAY FOR?

Make a list so that you can refer to it from time to time:

_____

_____

_____

_____

_____

_____

_____

_____

_____

_____

_____

_____

_____

_____

_____

_____

_____

_____

_____

_____

_____

_____

_____

_____

_____

_____

God Has Made Everything

Mountain peaks covered with snow
    Fertile valleys stretched below
Laden with fruit the trees continue to grow
    And the winding rivers flow

Silent lakes and gushing waterfalls
    God has made them all.

The sun in the sky shines so bright
    The moon high above with borrowed light
The twinkling stars, O! What a sight
    Beautiful day and beautiful night

Round in a cycle they do fall
    God has made them all

Fish living in water, animals with snouts
    Creatures of the deep that we know nothing about
Animals that squeak, animals that shout
    Everything is useful without any doubt

Animals that creep, animals that crawl
    God has made them all

The birds that fly, the birds that sing
    Beautiful flowers that blossom in Spring

You and me, the queen and the king
  God has created absolutely everything

Both black and white, both short and tall
  God has made them all

ACTIVITY

What is one of your favourite creations of God and why?

_____
_____
_____
_____
_____
_____
_____
_____
_____
_____
_____
_____
_____
_____
_____
_____
_____
_____
_____
_____
_____
_____
_____
_____

Jesus, may peace be on him

Jesus[as] was a Prophet of God,
    And Prophet of God was he
And all the Prophets were human beings
    They all lived like you and me.

Jesus[as] was a Prophet of God
    And Prophet of God was he
He rode a pony and walked on foot
    He travelled like you and me.

Jesus[as] was a Prophet of God
    And Prophet of God was he
When good news came he laughed with joy
    He laughed like you and me.

Jesus[as] was a Prophet of God
    And Prophet of God was he
When he was sad, he cried deep in his heart
    He cried like you and me.

Jesus[as] was a Prophet of God
    And Prophet of God was he
While on the cross he cried out loud
    Lord why hast thou forsaken me...

Jesus[as] was a Prophet of God
    And Prophet of God was he
God heard his prayers and saved him from death
    As he prayed in agony.

Jesus[as] was a Prophet of God
    And Prophet of God was he.
As he was in the fear of arrest again,
    He fled from his beloved Galilee.

Jesus[as] was a Prophet of God
    And Prophet of God was he
From place to place he travelled on foot
    Until he reached the Kashmir Valley.

Jesus[as] was a Prophet of God
    And Prophet of God was he
He lived in India for many years
    He lived there with his family.

Jesus[as] was a Prophet of God
    And Prophet of God was he
He completed his mission and passed away
    At the ripe old age of 120.

Jesus[as] was a Prophet of God
    And Prophet of God was he.
May his pious soul rest in peace
    Son of God he cannot be.

Jesus[as] was a Prophet of God
And Prophet of God was he.
This is the conclusion you arrive at
When you read his life history.

ACTIVITY

Circle the correct answer:

1. All prophets are human   TRUE   FALSE
2. Prophet Jesus was not put on the cross   TRUE   FALSE
3. Did Prophet Jesus, may peace be on him,
    complete his mission?   YES   NO
4. Prophet Jesus left Galilee and finally reached
                    QADIAN,   LONDON   KASHMIR
5. Prophet Jesus passed away at the age of:
                40   80   96,   100,   120,   136

If you are interested in learning more about Prophet Jesus' life you can read:

- *Jesus in India,* by the Promised Messiah[as]
- *Where did Jesus Die?,* by Jalal-ud-Din Shams[ra]
- *The True Story of Jesus,* by Rashid Ahmad Chaudhry

Lord of the Mighty Throne

Allah can see what you do
   He always watches over you

He is faithful as a Friend
   To help you His angels descend

He is super as a Guide
   In Him you can truly confide

He has power over everything
   The ferocious beast, the mightiest King

Ask from Him whatever you need
   Knock at His door and you will succeed

Believe in Him and seek His pleasure
   Allah is indeed the loveliest treasure

Who, when found by you or me
   Is like a strong boat in a stormy sea

Allah is sufficient for me
   Indeed there is no other God but He

We should worship him alone
   He is the Lord of the Mighty Throne

ACTIVITY

Allah has many names, you may have heard of the 99 Attributes of Allah. The verse of the Holy Quran that is repeated at the beginning of most surah's is:

بِسْمِ اللهِ الرَّحْمٰنِ الرَّحِيْمِ

Bismillaa hir-Rahmaanir-Raheem
In the Name of Allah, the Gracious, the Merciful.

Which Attributes of Allah can you find in this verse?

1. _____
   _____
   _____

2. _____
   _____
   _____

Can you explain each of these Attributes in your own words?

_____
_____
_____
_____
_____
_____

**COLOUR IN THE ARABIC CALLIGRAPHY THAT SAYS
'ALLAH'.**

الله

Our Leader (may peace and blessings of Allah be upon him)

Behold our leader
    Muhammad^{saw} is his name
We love him so dearly
    And worldwide is his fame.

He removed the darkness
    From the corners of the earth
Excellent is his example
    To follow from birth.

Holy are all Prophets
    Though their ranks not the same
The Holiest Muhammad^{saw}
    The beauty in his name!

He brought us the religion
    That lives on strong today
Islam, peace and submission
    A promise to obey.

The last to bring us a Law
    King of all who have already been
That is why we call him
    'Khaatamun-Nabiyeen'.

ACTIVITY

Ask someone older than you—your mum, dad, brother, sister, aunt, uncle, cousin etc., to tell you a story from the life of the Holy Prophet, may peace and blessings of Allah be upon him. If you cannot find someone to tell you a story, you can always search on www.alislam.org.

Write down the story in your own words:

_____
_____
_____
_____
_____
_____
_____
_____
_____
_____
_____
_____
_____
_____
_____
_____
_____
_____

Prayer Is the Key to Paradise

Early in the morning, just before dawn
  A Mu'adhdhin from the mosque calls the Adhaan

From a minaret, his voice loud and clear
  He calls the believers from far and near

'Prayer is better than sleep,' he loudly declares
  Come to the mosque and leave behind your affairs

'Prayer leads to success,' he does then call
  O do come quickly now and do not stall

Hurry up and leave your comfortable bed
  And do get ready for Prayer instead

Prayer does help you to achieve your goal
  It is indeed a tonic for the soul

Perform ablutions, gather in the hall
  Let not Satan allure you ever at all

Join the worshippers and follow the Imam
  Through Ruku, Sajdah, Qa'adah and Qiyaam

Ask everything from your Lord, your God
No matter how small, or even how odd!

Importance of Prayer, you must realise
It is the secret key to Paradise.

ACTIVITY

Sometimes friends that are not Muslim might think it is crazy that you pray five times a day! But you can prove to them that the five daily prayers do not take up much time at all! For one day ask an adult to record how long you spend.

_____
_____
_____
_____
_____
_____
_____

- Playing _____hours_____mins
- Eating _____hours_____mins
- Watching TV _____hours_____mins
- Browsing internet _____hours_____mins
- Other activities _____hours_____mins
- Praying _____hours_____mins

Out of 24 hours, how long do you spend praying? _____

You see!! The five daily prayers do not take up much time at all!

The Girl with Swollen Eyes

A little girl had swollen eyes
    And she was in terrible pain
She went to many doctors
    But it was all in vain.

One day she met the Promised Messiah[as]
    And requested him to pray
'Holiness,' she said to him
    'I'm in pain night and day.'

The Messiah[as] took pity on her
    When he saw her reddened face
Tenderly he spoke to her
    And slowed down his pace.

He put his finger in his mouth
    And rubbed it on her eyes
He then prayed to his Lord
    To Allah, the Mighty, the Wise.

After a while she felt better
    And the pain did really cease
She lived on for many years
    And never again had eye disease.

ACTIVITY

Fill in the gaps using the boxes from the table below this passage:

The girl had _____ _____.
This caused her _____ _____.
Although she had been to many _____,
none were able to _____ her. She asked the
_____ _____ to _____
for her. The _____ _____ took
pity on her. The _____ _____
put his _____ in his _____ and
gently rubbed it on her _____. Then he
_____ to _____. After some time
the girl felt _____. Never again did she have an
_____ _____!

Use each box once:		
better	prayed	finger
eyes	eye disease	terrible pain
mouth	Promised Messiah[as]	Allah
Promised Messiah[as]	swollen eyes	Promised Messiah[as]
doctors	cure	pray

40

The Month of Fasting Has Begun

The moon has been sighted
    Everyone is delighted
It will be lots of fun
    The month of fasting has begun.

Breakfast just before dawn
    Reciting the Holy Quran
Till the rising of the sun
    The month of fasting has begun.

No food during the day
    No visits to the café
No work will be left undone
    The month of fasting has begun.

No drinking, no eating
    Absolutely no cheating!
All the evils we will shun
    The month of fasting has begun.

One should never forget
    To break the fast at sunset.
God's pleasure will be won
    The month of fasting has begun.

At night an extra prayer
   Which puts us in the right gear
To goodness we always run
   The month of fasting has begun.

In the mosque we do pray
   For as long as we can stay
Heaven's door is closed to none
   The month of fasting has begun.

The moon is sighted again
   All are delighted again
For the day of Eid is tomorrow
   For Satan; what a day of sorrow.

ACTIVITY

The month of fasting is a special and spiritual time for Muslims. Although children do not fast, you can use this month to improve yourself by having targets. For example your target could be 'to be nice to my brother / sister'. Sticking to your target for the whole month, should help you do so throughout the year.

My target for this Ramadan is: _____

_____

_____

_____

_____

_____

_____

_____

_____

_____

_____

_____

_____

_____

_____

The Prophet^{saw} Has an Enemy

One day the Holy Prophet^{saw} was coming back
From the battlefield; the security was slack.

The sun was burning like a ball of fire
Every living thing was forced to retire.

He decided his men should rest a while
Under shady trees before another mile.

He hung his sword in the branches and lay
Unaware an enemy followed him all day.

The enemy moved close, took his sword from the tree
And said to him, 'who can save you from me?'

'Allah,' said the Prophet^{saw} without a trace of fear
The enemy dropped the sword, the Prophet^{saw} was near.

Then the Prophet^{saw} picked up the sword and said
'Now you tell me who can save you instead?'

'No one but you,' he cried with pleading eyes,
'Indeed you're always very kind and wise.'

'Very well,' said Prophet^{saw}, 'You're free to go.'
Allah is the saviour, of friend and foe.

ACTIVITY

1. What did the Holy Prophet^{saw} say when the enemy said: "who can save you from me?" _____
   _____

2. When the Holy Prophet said to the enemy: "Now you tell me who can save you instead?", what was the reply of the enemy? _____
   because_____
   _____
   _____
   _____
   _____
   _____
   _____
   _____
   _____

BONUS QUESTION: During which battle did the incident mentioned in the poem take place?

The incident took place during the Battle of _____.

Answers to Activities

True Muslims

Y	B	O	E		H	L	L	A	A		N	D	A
o	b	e	y		A	l	l	a	h		a	n	d

I	H	S		L	K	A	A	I	H	F	H	.
h	i	s		K	h	a	l	i	f	a	h	.

R	O	U		E	R	S	H	T	A
O	u	r		h	e	a	r	t	s

I	L	I	W		U	N	T	R		Y	A	A	W
w	i	l	l		t	u	r	n		a	w	a	y

R	M	O	F		K	S	N	D	E	A	S	R
f	r	o	m		d	a	r	k	n	e	s	s

D	A	N		L	S	V	E	I	.
a	n	d		e	v	i	l	s	.

The Promised Messiah,
may peace be on him

A	L	L	A	H	H	S	F	J	X	L	D	J	K	X	L	I
E	B	I	B	L	E	E	M	Q	V	F	A	U	J	H	Y	Z
M	F	A	V	P	N	R	E	G	U	T	M	S	W	K	H	M
O	S	I	D	N	M	U	C	Y	Q	R	H	T	B	W	P	M
N	A	U	L	A	H	T	L	R	A	J	A	D	F	X	U	L
T	D	N	N	H	I	P	I	L	K	E	M	N	B	H	N	V
H	L	Y	H	Q	M	I	P	I	Y	S	A	R	X	A	I	I
O	U	W	G	M	A	R	S	D	F	U	L	Q	L	I	Q	N
F	D	D	E	I	M	C	E	F	Y	S	U	W	A	S	U	D
F	T	A	N	H	M	S	D	N	A	P	H	R	U	S	E	L
A	W	Z	O	T	A	T	H	S	D	W	G	A	T	E	S	M
S	Q	P	O	P	H	N	X	S	V	E	N	U	I	M	X	H
T	D	Y	M	E	D	E	N	N	E	V	Z	A	R	E	N	I
I	S	R	H	C	I	I	Z	Z	N	W	N	Z	I	R	J	T
N	A	P	L	C	A	C	O	K	T	W	U	Z	P	D	Y	R
G	U	O	S	A	M	N	D	J	G	I	T	C	S	E	A	G
B	S	Q	D	U	G	A	P	J	C	E	H	B	E	O	H	Q

Jesus, may peace be on him

Circle the correct answer:

1. All prophets are human   TRUE
2. Prophet Jesus was not put on the cross   FALSE
3. Did Prophet Jesus, may peace be on him, complete his mission?   YES
4. Prophet Jesus left Galilee and finally reached   KASHMIR
5. Prophet Jesus passed away at the age of: 120

Lord of the Mighty Throne

بِسْمِ اللهِ الرَّحْمٰنِ الرَّحِيْمِ

Bismillaa hir-Rahmaanir-Raheem
In the Name of Allah, the Gracious, the Merciful.

Which Attributes of Allah can you find in this verse? The Attributes of Allah found in the verse بِسْمِ اللهِ الرَّحْمٰنِ الرَّحِيْمِ are:

1. رحمٰن *[Rahmaan—Gracious]*

2. رحيم *[Raheem—Merciful]*

The Girl with Swollen Eyes

Did you get all the words in **bold** in the correct order?

The girl had **swollen eyes**. This caused her **terrible pain**. Although she had been to many **doctors**, none were able to **cure** her. She asked the **Promised Messiah** to **pray** for her. The **Promised Messiah** took pity on her. The **Promised Messiah** put his **finger** in his **mouth** and gently rubbed it on her **eyes**. Then he **prayed** to **Allah**. After some time the girl felt **better!** Never again did she have an **eye disease!**

Publisher's Note

Salutations are recited out of respect when mentioning the names of Prophets and holy personages. These salutations have been abbreviated and inserted into the text where applicable.

Readers are urged to recite the full salutations for the following abbreviations:

saw   *sallallaahu 'alaihi wa sallam,* meaning 'peace and blessings of Allah be upon him', is written after the name of the Holy Prophet Muhammad[saw].

as   *'alaihis-salaam,* meaning 'peace be on him', is written after the names of Prophets other than the Holy Prophet Muhammad[saw].

ra   *raziyallaahu 'anhu/'anhaa/'anhum,* meaning 'Allah be pleased with him/her/them', is written after the names of the Companions of the Holy Prophet Muhammad[saw] or of the Promised Messiah[as].

rta   *rahmatullaah 'alaihi/'alaihaa/'alaihim,* meaning 'Allah shower His mercy upon him/her/them', is written after the names of those deceased pious Muslims who are not Companions of the Holy Prophet Muhammad[saw] or of the Promised Messiah[as].

Notes

This book belongs to

_____

_____

_____

_____